KIDSPLAY

For Adam

Childhood is not from birth to a certain age ...
        ... and at a certain age
The child is grown, and puts away childish things.
Childhood is the kingdom where nobody dies.
Nobody that matters, that is.

Edna St Vincent Millay

KIDSPLAY

John Lee

Cambridge University Press

CAMBRIDGE

NEW YORK   NEW ROCHELLE   MELBOURNE   SYDNEY

ACT NOW PLAYS

Series editor: Peter Rowlands
Founding editor: Andrew Bethell

Roots, Rules and Tribulations Andrew Bethell
Closed Circuit Mike English
Faust and Furious Anne Lee
Czechmate Gerry Docherty and Bill Kinross
Spring Offensive Ray Speakman and Derek Nicholls
Football Apprentices David Holman
Gregory's Girl Bill Forsyth
Vacuees Bill Martin
Easy on the Relish Andrew Bethell
Fans Mike English
Three Minute Heroes Leslie Stewart
Wednesday's Child Tony Higgins
The Tree that holds up the Sky Paul King
The Fourth Year are Animals Richard Tulloch
Fit for Heroes Charlie Moritz
Do we ever see Grace? Noël Greig
Rainbow's Ending Noël Greig
Kidsplay John Lee
Terms of Engagement Martin Dimery

Published by the Press Syndicate of the University of Cambridge
The Pitt Building, Trumpington Street, Cambridge CB2 1RP
32 East 57th Street, New York, NY 10022, USA
10 Stamford Road, Oakleigh, Melbourne 3166, Australia

First published 1989

Printed in Great Britain by
David Green Printers Ltd, Kettering, Northamptonshire

British Library Cataloguing-in-Publication Data
Lee, John
Kidsplay. — (Act Now)
I. Title II. Series
822′.914

ISBN 0 521 36946 0

US

Performance

KIDSPLAY

Kidsplay was first performed by Hull Truck Youth Theatre at Spring Street Theatre, Hull in April 1984 under the title of *Ten-Foot Kids*. The original cast was as follows:

MICHAEL John Collins
MARTIN Phil Higginson
SHANE Mike Farmery
CHARLIE Donna McKenzie
JENNY Abigail French
ROBYN Cathy Peace
MELANIE Rozi Lister
BRIAN Paul McIlvaney
KEITH Neil Pinnock
JOHN Andy Wheller
NIGEL Martin Bailie
LUCY Suzanne Williams
RACHEL Alison Welpton
KATIE Sally Ann Cole
JOANNA Vickie Mills
GEORGE Mark Rudland
MAGGIE Madeline Bronfield
SAM Joanne Dent
PENNY Helen Greendale
WILLIE Lee Bradley
VAL Helen Johnson
ANGELA Sarah Hawkins
NICOLA Fiona Whitley

Additional characters in the original version were played by:

Sarah Ward   Cheryl Flitton
Erica Fudge   Mandi Padamsee
Emma King   Mike Smith
Sally Booth   Lee Scott

CHARACTERS

MICHAEL (10)	Likeable, cheeky, everybody's friend.
MARTIN ($11\frac{1}{2}$)	Michael's brother. Tries to act grown up – usually fails.
SHANE (10)	Michael's friend and neighbour. Young for his age.
CHARLIE ($10\frac{3}{4}$)	Shane's big sister. Sensible girl. Likes Martin.
JENNY (11)	Friendly, popular girl. Charlotte's best friend.
ROBYN (10)	Independent. A bit of a 'tomboy'.
MELANIE (11 today!)	Sweet and pretty. Not allowed to play in the alley.
BRIAN (9)	Lives at the bottom of the street. Scruffy. A 'loner'.
KEITH (9)	A bit unsure of his position in the gang.
JOHN (9)	Keith's cousin from London.
NIGEL (8)	Robyn's little brother. Dominated by her.
LUCY (8) RACHEL (7)	Younger girls on the block.
KATIE (8) JOANNA (7)	Have to be in earlier than the others.

Melanie's party guests

GEORGE (11)	A big boy. Throws his weight about.
MAGGIE (10)	George's sister. Wears glasses.
SAM (9)	George's little sister.
PENNY (nearly 12!)	Maturing quickly. Beginning to find boys interesting.
WILLIE (11)	Penny's brother. A bit soppy. Enjoys dance class.
VAL (10)	Penny and Willie's friend. Quiet, nice girl.
ANGELA (9)	Plain, polite girl.
NICOLA (8)	Angela's sister. Very shy. Cries easily.

Grown-ups

MELANIE'S MUM SHANE'S MUM MICHAEL'S DAD	Voices heard off-stage.

A NOTE ON PRODUCTION

The scene remains the same throughout the play – a narrow stretch of back-alley behind a block of houses which is referred to as a 'ten-foot' in the play. It is as wide as the stage or the performing area is deep and continues off both sides. At the back there is an assortment of fences, wall and garages with three gates leading into back gardens. The middle fence has a street-lamp in front of it and is distinctly ramshackle in appearance. The gate has '23' painted on it and leads to Michael and Martin's garden. The gate on the left of this, number 21, leads to Charlie and Shane's. The right-hand gate has no number and leads to Melanie's garden. Her gate and wall are noticeably smarter than the others.

Alternatively, the whole play can be performed on a bare space, though some minimum of drapes or screens would be needed to suggest the three upstage entrances. The central-streep lamp is a focal gathering place for the kids as street-lamps always are. It can also be quite simply represented, but for performance the atmosphere at the end of the play is greatly enhanced if working light can be arranged.

The real dramatic interest, however, lies in the coming and going of the 23 'kids' and the story that unfolds as they interact. Their language should be vivid enough to bring them quickly to life on a simple reading. Any group attempting to perform the play, though, would be well advised to spend some preparatory time in improvisation work developed from observing, and remembering, just how smaller children move, stand, speak, laugh, cry and, above all, *play*. The dramatic challenge for older actors lies in convincingly portraying characters several years younger than themselves. We've all been there!

STAGE DIRECTIONS

There are two kinds of directions in this playscript. Those in **bold type** provide information that is essential to an understanding of what is happening in the play at the time. For a play-reading, these should be read by a separate reader.

Those in *italic type* are less essential stage directions and offer suggestions to assist with a production of the play on stage. In a reading they are best not read out as they will hamper the flow of the play, although those who are reading may find that some of these instructions offer help with the interpretation of their lines.

ACT ONE

BEFORE TEA

As the lights come up, JOANNA is bouncing a ball on one side while three girls are skipping in front of the street-lamp. They are all about eight years old. RACHEL is in the middle. As LUCY and KATIE swing the rope they chant:

LUCY When this song comes to an end

KATIE Tell us the name of your boyfriend.
A ... B ... C ... D ...

(On 'D' LUCY gives the rope a jerk and catches RACHEL's foot.)

LUCY D!! Err ... You go out with Derek!

RACHEL No I don't, then!

KATIE Yes you do! You go out with Derek – it said so!

RACHEL No it didn't! Anyway, you pulled the rope up on purpose! Cheat!

LUCY No I didn't!

RACHEL Yes you did. You cheated and you've got to do it again.

JOANNA *(Coming over)* No you're not. It's my go now! C'mon!

LUCY I'm fed up with this game.

KATIE Shall we play horses?

LUCY Yeah! I'll be a horse!

JOANNA I don't want to be a horse!

KATIE I'll be a puller with Rachel.

LUCY I'll be called 'Chestnut'.

JOANNA What can I be?

LUCY You be called ... err ... 'Peanut'! Come on!

(With some protest from JOANNA, she and LUCY put the rope over their shoulders. RACHEL and KATIE take the 'reins'. They begin cantering around with suitable noises. Suddenly, BRIAN appears from the side on his BMX bike with his siren going. He ploughs through the girls, making aeroplane and gun noises.)

LUCY You go away, Brian Sullivan and stop spoiling our game!

BRIAN Err, I shot you all – you're all dead!

KATIE No we're not. Get lost!

BRIAN I can beat you lot any day!

JOANNA Come on! Let's tie him up!

(The girls run around BRIAN with the skipping rope, tying him up.)

BRIAN Arr! Gerroff! Stop it!

LUCY Err, he's going to start crying.

BRIAN I'll tell me mam!

JOANNA Hit him!

(LUCY hits BRIAN. He falls over.)

BRIAN You've had it now! I will tell me mam ... and I mean it!

KATIE Go on then, we don't care ... big baby!

LUCY He's crying! Cry baby! Cry baby!

(The girls continue to taunt BRIAN while he struggles to unravel himself. Finally, he manages to do so and holds the rope in his hand.)

BRIAN Ha! I've got your skipping rope now!

JOANNA Give it me back!

BRIAN You get back or else I'll hit you! *(Threatening her with the rope)* And I'm not joking either ... 'cos I'm going to throw it over the wall into that graveyard with all the bogeymen ... *(Indicating audience)*.

LUCY No! Don't, Brian!

BRIAN I will. I'll throw it in the cemetery and the bogeymen'll get it and ...

RACHEL Orr, don't Brian. We're not allowed to go in there and we won't get it back.

BRIAN Well ... only if you'll play with me then.

GIRLS Yeah, alright.
Right.
OK.

BRIAN Say 'Promise', 'cos I don't believe you!

GIRLS *(More or less together)* Cross my heart, hope to die
Stick a needle in my eye!
Promise! *(They have fingers crossed behind their backs.)*

JOANNA Give us it back then.

BRIAN After a hundred then ... Ready? ... One, two ... miss a few ... ninety-nine, *hundred*! *(He throws the rope down.)*

GIRLS Naaah! We had our fingers crossed!

KATIE We've got to go in now anyway ... who wants to play with you!

(The GIRLS all run off, jeering at BRIAN, who is left angry and upset.)

BRIAN You dirty cheaters! You said you'd play with me!

(In desperation, BRIAN blows a rude noise after them and stamps the floor. He starts to walk back to his bike, mumbling and cursing. MICHAEL's head suddenly appears over

his fence at the back – he is standing on his rabbit-hutch. He pulls a pin out of an imaginary grenade and lobs it at Brian.)

MICHAEL Yeeow! *(He makes explosion noises.)*

(BRIAN **immediately reacts with a burst of machine-gun-fire.)**

MICHAEL Yarr! I blew you up! You're dead now!

BRIAN No you didn't 'cos I got out of the way just in time and I shot you as well, so you're dead!

MICHAEL No you didn't! I killed you first over there.

BRIAN You didn't 'cos I'm stood over here and anyway I'm Superboy and bombs can't hurt me!

BRIAN No you're not then, 'cos I blew you up!

BRIAN Anyway, do you want to come out and play with me out here and we can have a really good game ...

MICHAEL Orr ... No ... I can't. Anyway, I've got to go now 'cos I'm on a secret mission. See ya! *(He extends his arms and 'flies' down behind the fence.)*

(BRIAN **is again left stamping his foot and making rude noises. He crosses to his bike and starts to leave. As he does so, the left-hand gate (number 21) opens.** CHARLIE **and** JENNY **appear with dollies, tea set, blanket, etc.)**

CHARLIE Close the gate.

JENNY Alright.

(CHARLIE **and** JENNY **proceed to lay out the blanket and tea set.** BRIAN **has stopped to watch.)**

JENNY Right – you look after that baby and I'll look after this one. Do you want a cup of tea?

CHARLIE Yes, please.

(BRIAN **leaps over and sits down between them.)**

BRIAN *Yes please!* I want a cup of tea!

JENNY Go away, Brian Sullivan!

CHARLIE We don't want you to play with us. Anyway, you're not invited to our party.

JENNY Yeah, we don't want a boy! Yeeach!

BRIAN I'll be daddy, you be mummy and you be sister.

CHARLIE No! We don't *need* a daddy! Go away!

BRIAN *(Snatching a dolly)* Come 'ere naughty baby and get a smack ...

CHARLIE Gerroff my dolly!

JENNY *Brian*! I'm gonna get really mad in a minute if you don't go away.

CHARLIE Yeah, she'll get really mad at you.

JENNY And you haven't seen me when I'm ever so mad!

CHARLIE No! *(Brian is quiet.)* Right ... You have the white cup and I'll have the red cup ... no, I'll have the white cup ...

BRIAN And I'll have the red cup!

JENNY Will you go away, Brian Sullivan? Go and play in your own bit.

CHARLIE Orr ... Can I have a cup of tea now, Jenny?

BRIAN Alright. *(Lifting teapot)* 'Ere you are then!

JENNY Brian! I'm warning you!

CHARLIE Oh, make him go away, Jenny.

JENNY Are you gonna be quiet?

BRIAN Yeah.

JENNY Right then ... I'll pour the tea ...

BRIAN *(Snatching cup back)* And I'll drink it!

JENNY Brian Sullivan! Will you ... *bugger off*!!

(There is a stunned silence. BRIAN **drops the cup.** CHARLIE **is shocked.)**

BRIAN *(Running to his bike)* I'm gonna get you into trouble!

JENNY Orr! I didn't mean it Brian!

BRIAN I'm gonna tell on you!

(BRIAN **rushes off.)**

CHARLIE *(Quite upset)* I'll have to go in now Jenny, 'cos I'll get into trouble if my mam knows you've said that!

JENNY I didn't mean it, honest! Don't go in yet, Charlie.

CHARLIE Right, well ... we're going to play 'houses' now.

JENNY Yeah and it's my house and I'm called Mrs Smith.

CHARLIE Alright and I will be Mrs Jones ...

JENNY No, I want to be called Mrs Jones!

CHARLIE Oh ... alright.

JENNY And you have to knock on my door.

CHARLIE Alright.

JENNY Do you want me to answer it?

CHARLIE No, I'll come in myself.

JENNY And this is my kitchen.

CHARLIE Alright!

JENNY Alright.

(CHARLIE **mimes knocking on the door while stamping her foot.)**

CHARLIE Hello Mrs Jones, it's Mrs Smith. Can I come in, please?

JENNY Oh hello Mrs Smith. Yes you can come in.

(ROBYN **enters from down the alley.)**

JENNY Hiya, Robyn!

ROBYN Hiya!

CHARLIE You can play parties with us now, Robyn. I know ... *(to Jenny)* You will be mammy and I will be big sister and *(to Robyn)* you can be daddy 'cos you haven't got one, have you?

(ROBYN shows she is very hurt by this suggestion but says nothing.)

JENNY I'll be called ... Tracey!

CHARLIE Alright.

JENNY No! No! ... Debbie! No ... Vickie! That's it!

ROBYN I *have* got a daddy then!

CHARLIE No you haven't then!

JENNY 'Cos I know you haven't!

ROBYN Yes I have then!

CHARLIE Who!

ROBYN My mummy's my daddy!

CHARLIE That's daft!

ROBYN No it's not! My mummy's my daddy and my mummy.

CHARLIE Well ... well, you just go home now and get your dolly.

ROBYN I haven't got a dolly.

JENNY You haven't got a dolly? All little girls have got dollies!

ROBYN Well I haven't.

CHARLIE Well maybe you're not a little girl then ... maybe you're a little boy!

ROBYN *(Shouting)* Yes I am a girl then! My brother Nigel's a boy and I'm a girl and my mummy's my mummy ... and my daddy!

CHARLIE Well ... well that just shows you don't know the difference between boys and girls then, dun't it?

JENNY Yeah, it does!

CHARLIE *(Beginning to snigger a bit)* And we do, don't we?

JENNY Yeah, I'm gonna tell her!

CHARLIE No! Let me!

JENNY Go on then.

CHARLIE The difference between boys and girls is ...

JENNY Go on!

CHARLIE The difference between boys and girls is ... that ... boys ... are ... daddies and girls are mummies!!

ROBYN Well, I knew that anyway ... everybody knows that. That not the *real* difference!

CHARLIE Well, what's the real difference then?

ROBYN Boys can wee standing up! *(Explosion of giggles)*

JENNY Orr, they do, don't they! ... Hey! Hey, but I know a bigger difference than that.

CHARLIE Go on then ...

JENNY No, but I'm not telling you.

CHARLIE Orr, go on. We won't tell anybody.

JENNY Alright then. Well ... when girls grow up and are big girls ...

CHARLIE Yeah ... *(Sniggers)* Go on!

JENNY When girls grow and are big girls ... *(More stifled giggles)* They have to ... They have to ... *(Sniggers and giggles)*

CHARLIE Go o-on!!

JENNY They have to wear bras! *(Jenny and Charlie burst out laughing.)*

ROBYN No they don't!

JENNY, CHARLIE *Yes they do!*

ROBYN My mummy doesn't!

CHARLIE *(Sniggering again)* Doesn't your mammy have any ... any ... boosoms!

ROBYN Yeah, she does, 'cos I've seen 'em when she runs!

CHARLIE Yeeurgh! That's horrible!

JENNY Hey! I know another difference! I know another difference! It's even bigger than that one ... But it's even ruder so I'm not saying it!

CHARLIE Orr, go on!

JENNY No!

CHARLIE Go on! Say it, go on!

JENNY Well ... the difference between boys and girls is that boys have got ... *(Sniggers begin again.)*

ROBYN Say it! You daren't ... go on!

JENNY Boys ... have ... got ... *(Charlie can hardly contain herself.)*

CHARLIE *Go on!!*

JENNY Boys have got ... short hair and girls have long hair! Like me! *(She waves her pigtail.)*

ROBYN *(Grabbing Jenny's hair and pulling it)* I don't want long hair!

JENNY Oww! ... YOU ... ROTTEN PIG! *(She smacks Robyn.)*

CHARLIE Well ... *all* boys are horrible, anyway.

JENNY Yeah, they smell and they've got fleas and nits!

CHARLIE And dicks!

ROBYN Yeah, I know, 'cos Brian Sullivan's got dicks 'cos he always has to stay behind when he goes to see Nitty Nora!

CHARLIE Nitty Nora, the bug explorer! *(Laughter)* I tell you what ... the only nice boys in the world are if you've got a boyfriend.

JENNY Yeah.

CHARLIE *(To Jenny)* Have you got one?

JENNY *(Hesitant)* No-o ... but I might have tomorrow!

CHARLIE *(To Robyn)* Have you got one?

ROBYN I might have. I'm not telling.

CHARLIE You haven't have you? Well I have, 'cos my boyfriend lives there 'cos Martin's my boyfriend.

(MICHAEL's head suddenly appears over his fence.)

MICHAEL No he isn't though! 'Cos Martin's my brother and he's not your boyfriend!

CHARLIE He-ey! You shouldn't be eardropping!

MICHAEL Well ... I can't help it can I, 'cos I'm ten-foot tall!

CHARLIE No you're not then ... you're standing on your rabbit-hutch!

MICHAEL Well I aren't then, clever, 'cos it's not a rabbit-hutch. It's a *ferret*-hutch now, so there!

JENNY Well, what happened to Snowy the rabbit?

MICHAEL It ... It died.

CHARLIE Orr ... Did you bury it?

MICHAEL No, we ate it!

CHARLIE Eerrgh!

ROBYN Did you have to kill it yourself?

CHARLIE Shurrup! I bet Martin didn't eat any, did he?

MICHAEL He did though ... me dad told him it was chicken. Anyway, ferrets are better than rabbits 'cos they can do tricks!

ROBYN No they can't

MICHAEL Yes they can. They can fly!

ROBYN No they can't!

MICHAEL Yes they can ... if you throw 'em off the roof!

CHARLIE Orr, that's horrible. *(Robyn finds it very funny.)*

MICHAEL Anyway Charlotte, is your Shane coming out to play?

CHARLIE I don't know. Do you want to play parties with us?

ROBYN Yeah, you can be daddy – they need a daddy.

MICHAEL Orr, no, I can't see, 'cos me mum told me I've got to clean me ferret out.

ROBYN Can I come and watch?

MICHAEL No! See ya! *(He disappears.)*

(JENNY leaps up from her sitting position.)

JENNY Oorrrrgh! I've sat in something wet!

CHARLIE It'll be a puggle.

JENNY Orr, me bum's wet, Charlotte! *(She sticks it in Charlie's direction.)*

CHARLIE Gerraway! Don't!!

JENNY Robyn, me bum's all wet ... look! *(She points it at Robyn.)*

ROBYN Giyup ... I don't want to see it!

(SHANE suddenly bursts through his gate (number 21) with a home-made bow and arrow.)

SHANE I'm gonna *shoot* yer! I'm Robin Hood and I've got the biggest and bestest bow and arrow in the whole world ... and I've got some merry men in my garden ... but ... they can't come out to play 'cos they've been very naughty ... 'specially Friar Tuck!

ROBYN Why aren't you playing with the other boys?

(SHANE is baffled by this question and slowly lowers his bow.)

CHARLIE Yeah!

(CHARLIE goes over and smacks SHANE. He drops his bow. ROBYN also stomps over and wallops him. He starts to cry and sniff.)

CHARLIE He-ey! *You* can't hit him!

SHANE No, you can't him me ... only my sister can hit me!

CHARLIE You sit down now and behave yourself ... and tuck yourself in!

JENNY Yeah, you have to play babies for that!

SHANE No! I don't want to play babies!

(JENNY thrusts a dolly into SHANE's hands.)

CHARLIE I know, we will play mammies and daddies.

JENNY Yeah, we've got a daddy now, haven't we?

SHANE No I'm Robin Hood!

CHARLIE No you're not. ... and it's time for baby to go to bed and she has to go on her potty ...

SHANE I think I can hear me merry men calling me!

CHARLIE No you can't! So you have to take her tights and her knickers off to put her on the potty.

SHANE *(Deeply distressed)* Orr, no ... I don't know how to do it! I don't know how to do it!

CHARLIE Hold her!

JENNY I'll show you how to do it, easy. You put her head between your legs like this ... and you pull her knickers off like that and then you sit her on her potty. *(She uses a party bowl.)*

CHARLIE That's it. She's doing it, look ...

JENNY And you have to let them sit there for a bit till they've finished.

SHANE I don't wanna!

CHARLIE Look, there it is. You take them down now!

SHANE It's rude!

CHARLIE No it isn't.

SHANE Somebody might see!

JENNY No they won't.

SHANE She'll get a cold bum!

CHARLIE Orr, look, she's got to have one or she'll wet the bed. Now go on! *(To Jenny)* Has she finished now? *(Lifts baby off.)*

JENNY Yeah! *(They look at it.)* She's done well, hasn't she? Who's a clever little mammy's baby then, eh?

CHARLIE That's good isn't it? *(She slings the 'contents' away.)*

SHANE I've done it now.

CHARLIE And the knickers!

JENNY Go on! Hurry up!

(SHANE tries not to look but his curiosity gets the better of him once he's got the knickers off.)

SHANE She 'asn't got no bum!

JENNY Yes she has – there!

CHARLIE You stop looking and put her on her potty now!

(SHANE throws the baby in the general direction of the potty.)

CHARLIE Hey! Stupid!

SHANE Well, I don't know how to do it, do I?

CHARLIE She's crying now! You've got to sing her a lullaby now.

SHANE *(Becoming desperate)* I don't know how to sing a lullaby!

JENNY 'Rock-a-bye baby on the treetops ...' There you are!

SHANE I can't sing!

CHARLIE Go on!

(SHANE pauses, then suddenly launches into 'Spiderman, Spiderman' or whatever, while jigging the baby up and down in the air.)

GIRLS Nooo-o!

SHANE Well I can't sing, can I, I told you!

CHARLIE Well if he can't sing, he'll just have to kiss her goodnight, won't he?

SHANE *(In panic)* No! I don't wanna kiss her!

JENNY Yeah, you've got to kiss her ... Now!

SHANE Hang on, hang on, she's telling me summat! *(Holding the baby to his ear)* She says she wants a chocolate biscuit for her supper before she goes to bed.

CHARLIE Well we haven't got any chocolate biscuits ... we've only got ginger biscuits.

SHANE She's telling me she wants a ginger biscuit!

JENNY No! You've still got to kiss her!

(JENNY decides to use force. During the ensuing struggle, MICHAEL appears through his gate.)

MICHAEL Shane! What y' doing?

SHANE *(Leaping up)* Nothing! I wasn't doing nothing!

CHARLIE He's been kissing our baby.

SHANE *No*! I wasn't!

MICHAEL Err! You big puff!!

SHANE I wasn't kissing her baby anyway. She's fibbing. That's why her bum's so big, 'cos she's always fibbing.

CHARLIE You big liar!

SHANE Anyway, what you doing, Michael?

MICHAEL I came to ask you if you want to clean my ferret out with us.

SHANE Can I?

MICHAEL Yeah, I asked me mam – she said you can. Come on!

(ROBYN stands up. She has been quietly dismantling the bow and arrow and has tied it into a cross.)

ROBYN Hey, Shane, before you go ... do you want your bow and arrow back?

SHANE Oh yeah, give us it ... I nearly forgot it!

ROBYN *(Pulling it from behind her back)* It's a kite!

SHANE *(Nearly crying)* Look what she's done to my bow and arrow!

ROBYN You only need to put some paper over it and you can fly it.

SHANE I don't *want* a kite. What'll me merry men say?

MICHAEL It doesn't matter anyway, 'cos we can mend it and we've got loads of sticks, so we can make a better one if we want.

SHANE Yeah, we can make a better one, see! And when we come out we're gonna shoot you all dead! *(They start to leave.)*

CHARLIE Well, you just make sure you're in for your tea.

SHANE Shurrup, baba-brain! *(The gate slams shut.)*

CHARLIE He-ey ... I'll tell my mam on him!

JENNY I know! Let's bake a cake.

ROBYN I'll make it! *(She grabs the bowl.)*

CHARLIE No, no ... wipe the wee-wee out first! *(Robyn does so.)* Now put the things in it. That's right. Now put the lid on. And put it in the oven.

ROBYN Where's the oven?

(KEITH and JOHN suddenly run on from down the alley.)

CHARLIE Hey, Keith, who's that?

KEITH It's my cousin John from London. We've gorra hide 'cos we're playing hide 'n' seek, and *(to Robyn)* your brother Nigel's after us!

ROBYN I know where you can hide. You can get under this blanket and be a table!

(CHARLIE and JENNY protest, but ROBYN is already lifting the blanket up and shoving the boys down on hands and knees and covering them. KEITH's head faces front, JOHN's the other way. The girls begin to arrange the pots and themselves on the 'Table'. We hear NIGEL calling.)

NIGEL *(Off-stage)* Coming ready or no-ot!

(NIGEL comes running on.)

CHARLIE He's here! ... Would you like a cup of tea, Mrs Jones?

JENNY Yes thank you, Mrs Smith, I would like a cup of tea.

NIGEL I can see you, Keith and John, I know you're there.

ROBYN Why are you talking to a table, stupid?

NIGEL I know there's Keith and John under there. Anyway, you big fat cheaters, you weren't supposed to go past *that* lamp-post *(pointing off)* not this one.

ROBYN Don't know what you're talking about ... we're playing parties.

(KEITH sticks his head out front, strains hard and loudly breaks wind. *(JOHN provides sound effects of farting from under blanket.)* **There is a slight pause, then John leaps up, upsetting everybody.)**

GIRLS Errrrh!

JOHN Oooh, you did it right up my nose!

(General chaos, laughter, wafting of blanket, etc.)

KEITH I couldn't help it!

(MICHAEL and SHANE suddenly burst out of the gate and ambush everybody with machine-guns. A full-scale war breaks out. As the madness subsides, MELANIE appears from her gate (right).)

MELANIE My mummy says you've got to be QUIET!

CHARLIE Wha-at?

MELANIE My mummy says you've got to be quiet.

JENNY Why?

MELANIE Because it's my birthday today and I'm eleven and I'm having a party in my garden.

ROBYN Can I come? I'll give you a present.

MELANIE No, it's only people from my dance class that are allowed to come – and mummy says you've got to leave them alone when they come to the back gate.

JENNY Well, why don't your friends use the front door then?

MELANIE Because they're not allowed to walk on the carpet!

MELANIE'S MUM *(Off-stage)* Melanie! Come away from that dirty alley-way! At once!!

(MELANIE disappears and closes the gate. The others jeer after her.)

ALL Melanie, Smellanie ... Ner-er! *(And similar chants)*

SHANE Anyway, I don't care, 'cos I'm going to cubs after tea and do you know what I got for my birthday? I got a brand new cub knife and it's the best and most dearest one you can get and it's got this thing on it for ... well, I don't know what it's for but if you poke the cat with it, it runs away screaming like mad!

KEITH Hey! Can we see it?

SHANE Oh, no. Me mam says I can't bring it out, 'cos I might kill you all with it.

MICHAEL Hey, Shane, can we come in your garden and have a look at it?

SHANE Err ... yeah, but ... me mam says only one can come in at once.

(Cries of 'me! me!', etc.)

SHANE I'll do eeny-meeny then! *(They all line up.)* Eeny-meeny miney-mo ... I don't like you lot, so off we go!

(SHANE drags MICHAEL off through his gate. The others react accordingly.)

NIGEL *(To Keith and John)* Orr, come on you two – we're supposed to be playing hide 'n' seek. And it's your turn to be on, John, 'cos I saw you first ... Come on, Keith. *(They start to run off.)*

KEITH Yeah, ... and count up to a hundred ... and don't cheat!

(JOHN goes to the lamp-post, counts loudly, cheats a bit, then shouts.)

JOHN Coming ready or no-ot!

(MAGGIE and SAM appear, wearing party dresses and carrying presents. JOHN nearly collides with them as he starts to run off.)

MAGGIE Excuse me, but can you tell where the party is please?

JOHN *(Pointing to the dollies and running off)* 'Sthere!

JENNY Who are you two?

MAGGIE Excuse me, but can you please tell me where Melanie's party is?

JENNY Well ... that all depends which Melanie you're looking for, doesn't it – because I'm called Melanie and she's called Melanie ... and even Charlotte's called Melanie!

ROBYN Yeah, and even the teapot's called Melanie!

SAM No, Melanie from our dance class! You don't go to our dance class.

CHARLIE Hang on! How do we know you go to her dance class? 'Cos if you didn't and we told you where she lived, we'd get in trouble.

SAM Well, we never fib, do we?

MAGGIE No, we don't.

JENNY Well, you'll just have to prove it then!

CHARLIE Yeah!

SAM How can we prove it?

JENNY Yer can *dance*, can't yer?

MAGGIE Don't want to!

CHARLIE You'll just have to!

JENNY Right! So this is like a stage ... and she's the people watching.

ROBYN Yeah, and I sit with dolly and teddy and if you're good, I go 'Hooray!' and if you're bad, I go 'Boo, boo, boo!'

JENNY So now you have to dance, 'cos this is a stage.

SAM We've never done it in front of anybody before!

ROBYN Well, do it now then!

JENNY Hurry up! *(Maggie shuffles into position.)*

MAGGIE Are you ready?

(MAGGIE **performs a half-hearted step.)**

ROBYN Boo, boo, boo!

CHARLIE Yarr! That was rubbish, four-eyes *(To Sam)* It's your go now

SAM I can't do it!

CHARLIE Well, y' can't be any worse than your sister. Go on!

SAM Alright.

(SAM vaguely waves her arms.)

JENNY And y' legs!

(SAM does a quick step.)

ROBYN Boo! boo! boo!

JENNY Err, that was just *rubbish*!

MAGGIE Don't you call my sister's dancing rubbish, else we'll get our brother George onto you, and he's *this* big! *(Shows her)*

CHARLIE Well, where he is then?

SAM He's just gone to the shops to get Melanie a present!

CHARLIE Well, we don't care anyway, 'cos my boyfriend Martin only lives just there and he's *this* big! *(She jumps up.)*

MAGGIE Well, our brother George is really, really strong ...

SAM Yeah, George is cock of our school!

CHARLIE Well, my boyfriend Martin's heavyweight champion of the world!

SAM, MAGGIE No he isn't!

SAM Don't lie!

CHARLIE Yes he is!

ROBYN Anyway ... ! I think you ought to do it again, 'cos that wasn't enough anyway.

MAGGIE No!

SAM Well, see, we don't do it by ourselves – we all do it together don't we?

ROBYN Well, do it together then!

CHARLIE Yeah!

(SAM and MAGGIE prance about in vague formation. JENNY and CHARLIE help with the music. The dance finishes with beautiful curtseys. Jenny and Charlie hurl abuse at their efforts. ROBYN carries on providing the 'music' throughout as a slanging match develops, almost turning into a fight. SHANE and MICHAEL appear from Shane's gate. Shane crosses to Charlie. He tugs her sleeve. Nobody hears him.)

SHANE Mum says you've got to come in ...

CHARLIE *(To Robyn)* Shurrup!!

(ROBYN carries on for a few seconds more, then stops suddenly.)

CHARLIE *(To Shane)* What?

SHANE Mum says you've gorra come in now to have some tea and take me to cubs ... big gob!

CHARLIE Well I might not want to take you to cubs this week!

SHANE Well, she says there'll be trouble if you don't ... Din't she?

MICHAEL Err ... Yeah!

CHARLIE Orr, well ... You hold this then – here! *(Hands him dolly.)* Gerroff my blanket! *(She starts to gather things up.)*

SHANE *(To Michael)* Hey, look, this dolly's got no bum!

MAGGIE You shun't be looking up her skirt. Mucky pig!

SHANE *(Pulling knickers down)* Look!

MICHAEL Hee hee!

CHARLIE Stop it!

SHANE Well, mam says you should look after you own things. Din't she?

MICHAEL Err ... Yeah!

CHARLIE Well, he can't even cross the road by hisself!

SAM / MAGGIE } Our George can! *(Charlie shoves Shane towards the gate.)*

SHANE I can get half-way across by meself!

CHARLIE Go on in! 'Bye everybody then, 'bye!

(They exit to 'byes', etc.)

MICHAEL See ya, Shane!

JENNY Orr, Robyn, I'm going to call for Mary now ... are you coming?

ROBYN Yeah! Let's skip!

(JENNY and ROBYN exit, skipping. MICHAEL is left suddenly alone with MAGGIE and SAM. He is uncomfortable. They close in on him.)

MICHAEL Hiya!

SAM Do *you* know where the party is?

(MICHAEL shakes his head.)

MAGGIE Yes you do!

MICHAEL I don't.

SAM Where do you live?

MICHAEL *(Hesitating)* There.

SAM Melanie lives round here, doesn't she?

MAGGIE And if Melanie lives down here and you live there, you know where the party is, you fibber ... and if you don't tell us, I'm going to give you a big sloppy wet kiss!

SAM And I will hold your hand for ever and ever and never let go!

MICHAEL Orr, no, gerroff me hand! I'll tell me mam ... Let go!

(BRIAN runs on from down the alley.)

BRIAN Eerrgh! He's got some girlfriends!

(MICHAEL and the girls instantly separate themselves from each other.)

MICHAEL I haven't!

BRIAN You've been kissing, haven't yer?

MICHAEL No!! *(Sam and Maggie express equal disgust at the idea.)*

BRIAN You have 'cos I saw yer.

MICHAEL I haven't!

BRIAN When I was coming up there, you was giving 'em big kisses!

(MAGGIE and SAM close in on Brian and grab him from either side.)

MAGGIE Hey, kid, do you know where Melanie lives?

BRIAN No.

MAGGIE Yes you do!

SAM Go on ... tell us.

BRIAN I don't know!

(GEORGE appears from down the alley, carrying a package.)

SAM }
MAGGIE } Hiya George!

GEORGE Hiya! I've been to shops and I've bought a Star Wars book for Melanie. It's *ace* – I've been reading it

SAM Do you know ... that little kid's been really horrible to us and that big one's been trying to kiss us and touch us!

MICHAEL I haven't ... *honest*!

BRIAN He has! I saw him!

MICHAEL Shurrup, Brian!!

GEORGE Have you been kissing my sisters?

MICHAEL No, I haven't.

BRIAN Yes he has!

MICHAEL Brian! Shurrup!!

GEORGE Hey! What's that on your T-shirt?

(He points to MICHAEL's chest, as Michael looks down GEORGE lifts his hand and smacks him in the mouth.)

GEORGE Haa!

(MAGGIE and SAM cheer and jeer.)

GEORGE Orr, no, look ... I'm gonna make friends with him now.

BRIAN Yeah, you'd better – or he'll smack you, won't you, Michael?

MICHAEL Shurrup Brian!

GEORGE Here ... Shake!

(GEORGE holds out his hand. As MICHAEL puts his hand forward, George stabs him in the stomach.)

GEORGE Spear ...! Hey! I know you, don't I? You're called Tony Chestnut, aren't you?

MICHAEL No!

GEORGE Yes you are than! *Toe! Knee! Chest! Nut!*

(GEORGE smacks him in the appropriate place with each word.)

BRIAN Hey! Go and get your Martin!

MICHAEL Yeah! I'm going to get our Martin! *(He makes for his gate.)*

GEORGE Go and get him then!

MICHAEL I'm goin' to! And he's bigger than you!

GEORGE Oh yeah? I bet he's a big wimp then, like you!

MICHAEL I'm gonna tell him! He'll smash you! *Martin*!

(MICHAEL **exits.)**

BRIAN Go and get him, Michael ... Hurry up!

(GEORGE **and his sisters turn on** BRIAN**. He exits – rapidly. Insults are thrown after him.)**

GEORGE Come on, then, are we going to Melanie's party for some food or what? I'm starving!

SAM But we don't know where it is!

GEORGE Err ... thick-head. It's number twenty-five! That's twenny-one, and that twenny-three ... So that one must be twenny-five ... Come on!

(GEORGE **leads them over and knocks on Melanie's gate. They look at George's book and chatter until Melanie opens the gate.)**

MELANIE Hallo, George.

GEORGE Hiya, Melanie. Happy birthday! I've got you a present ...

MELANIE Oh, thank you.

SAM *(Giving her a present)* Happy birthday, Melanie.

MAGGIE *(Giving her a present)* Happy birthday, Melanie.

MELANIE Thank you all ever so much! Come in.

(They all exit, and there follows a slight pause. We hear more kids approaching. PENNY, VAL **and** WILLIE **appear. Willie is trailing behind.**

VAL Where *is* the party, though?

PENNY I don't know ... it's somewhere round here. What's Willie doing?

(WILLIE **enters, trailing his foot.)**

WILLIE Orr, I've got dog-cack on me shoe!

PENNY Oh, Willie! Wipe it off then!

WILLIE I can't!

PENNY Well, take your shoe off, then!

(WILLIE removes his shoe. They all look at it and go 'Yeeeurgh!' Willie cannot resist having a close-up sniff.)

WILLIE Poooh! It stinks! Smell it!

PENNY I can already smell it from here!

WILLIE *(Thrusting the shoe at Penny)* Smell it close! Go on!

PENNY Nooo-o! Take it away!

WILLIE I dare you to smell it!

PENNY No, I'm not going to smell it!

WILLIE Well ... Touch it then! Go on! You daren't.

VAL No! Don't!

(PENNY decides to touch it.)

PENNY Yeeurgh! Err, it's all yacky and squidgy!

VAL Orr, Penny! Err ... it's horrible!

PENNY What shall I do with it?

WILLIE Get Valerie to lick it off!!

VAL No! Take it away!

PENNY Orr, alright, I'll wipe it on this lamp-post.

WILLIE Yeeach! I hate ten-foots – they're horrible!

PENNY No, they're not ... they're good. I wish we had one!

WILLIE I don't! They're dirty and smelly and common ...

(MARTIN appears suddenly through his gate and crosses straight to WILLIE.)

MARTIN I'm gonna smack you!

WILLIE *(Leaping back in alarm)* What for?

PENNY *(Standing in front of Willie)* No, you're not!

MARTIN Yeah, I am. I'm gonna smack you!

WILLIE No you're not, then ... 'cos I'll rub dog-cacca up your nose!

PENNY Yeah! Go on, Willie!

(WILLIE thrusts the shoe at MARTIN's face. Martin backs off, squirming. Willie presses forward the attack.)

WILLIE *(Turning back)* He's running away, Penny! He's running away!

(MARTIN advances.)

WILLIE He's coming back, Penny! He's coming back!!

MARTIN I'm gonna really smack you for that now!

(WILLIE retreats and PENNY steps in front to protect him.)

PENNY Don't you *dare* touch my Willie!

(MARTIN can't prevent himself from bursting out laughing at this.)

MARTIN You 'aven't got a willie!

PENNY Don't be rude, you! That's my Willie!

WILLIE Yeah, and that's my Penny ... and that's my Valerie – well, she's not mine, cos she's not my sister ... but she's somebody's Valerie.

MARTIN I'm still gonna smack you!

WILLIE Why?

MARTIN 'Cos you've been shoving my brother about!

WILLIE No I haven't! I don't even know your brother!

PENNY No, we don't ... and anyway, Willie doesn't hit anybody, do you?

WILLIE No! We only just got here as well ... and I trod in this dog-cacca ... and I bet *you* did it!

PENNY Yeah! You're a dog!

WILLIE Yeah, you are! Woof, woof, woof!

(PENNY and VAL join in the barking and teasing. Meanwhile, CHARLIE opens her gate and comes out.)

MARTIN No I'm not a dog!

WILLIE Yes you are – you look like one!

CHARLIE *(Very affectionately)* Hiya Martin!

PENNY Who's that!

WILLIE That's your girlfriend, isn't it?

CHARLIE Yes!

MARTIN No!

PENNY Yes she is, then – she said so!

WILLIE Yaarrgh! He's got a girlfriend!

(SHANE has followed CHARLIE out. He is wearing his cub uniform. PENNY, WILLIE and VAL burst out laughing when they see him.)

PENNY Yarr, look! He's got ribbons in his socks!

WILLIE It's a Boy Sprout!

SHANE They're not ribbons, they're garters! It's me cub uniform!

PENNY What d'you wear garters for?

SHANE Er ... I dunno, but you've gorra wear 'em!

CHARLIE They're to hold your socks up, stupid!

SHANE Oh yeah! They're to hold me socks up ... see!

WILLIE That's stupid

CHARLIE What are you doing out here, Martin?

MARTIN I'm smacking that kid!

PENNY No you're not!

CHARLIE *Why?*

MARTIN 'Cos he's been shoving our Michael around.

CHARLIE No, he 'asn't!

PENNY See! Told you!

WILLIE Liar!

CHARLIE No, 'cos I saw your Michael come running in from my bedroom window and it was when them other lasses were here and it must have been their brother!

(MARTIN **stomps over to his gate and shouts.)**

MARTIN Michael! *Michael!!* Get out here!

SHANE There's a caccy smell round here ... and it's not me!

WILLIE It's on my shoe!

SHANE Pooh!

(MICHAEL **appears.** MARTIN **drags him towards** WILLIE. **He looks unhappy.)**

MARTIN Is that him?

MICHAEL Is that him what?

MARTIN Is that him what's been smacking you?

MICHAEL No.

(MARTIN **smacks** MICHAEL **across the head.)**

PENNY Hey! You shouldn't hit your brother!

(PENNY **smacks** MARTIN. **Martin raises his hand.)**

MARTIN Gerroff!

PENNY Don't you dare hit me else I'll scratch your eyes out!

WILLIE Yeah, she will an' all!

MARTIN Well I don't fight girls anyway!

PENNY That's 'cos I'd beat you, that's why!

MARTIN No it's not. It's 'cos me dad won't let me!

SHANE *(Tugging Charlie's sleeve)* Orr, come on Charlie, I'll be late for cubs!

CHARLIE Anyway, Martin, I'll have to go now ... 'cos he can't cross the road on his own yet. Me mam says I have to take him.

PENNY Orr, can't he?

WILLIE Big baby!

SHANE When I'm a sixer you won't be able to call me a baby. I'll be able to tell you what to do then!

PENNY Why? What are you now?

SHANE Err ... I'm nothing now ... But I soon will be!

CHARLIE Anyway, we've got to go now, Martin.

PENNY Kiss him goodbye then!

WILLIE Yeah, go on, kiss your girlfriend!

MARTIN No! She's not me girlfriend!

PENNY She says she is.

MICHAEL Yeah! You should kiss her for hitting me. Serves you right!

MARTIN Shurrup, you!

PENNY *Blow* him a kiss then!

SHANE Yeah, hurry up and blow him a kiss and let's go!

CHARLIE *(A little shyly)* Alright then.

(CHARLIE blows MARTIN a kiss.)

WILLIE Yaargh! It landed on your mouth!

(MARTIN spits and wipes his mouth in disgust. SHANE drags CHARLIE off.)

CHARLIE 'Bye, Martin! 'Bye everybody!

MICHAEL See ya, Shane!

PENNY Yeah, tara Sha-ane ... See y' when you're a sixer!!

(PENNY, WILLIE and VAL explode with laughter at this. CHARLIE and SHANE exit. PENNY crosses to MARTIN.)

PENNY Do you know where a girl called Melanie lives?

VAL From our dance class. She's got blonde hair.

PENNY Yeah, and she says her back gate's round here, opposite the graveyard there *(pointing to the audience)* but we don't know which is her gate.

WILLIE And she's having a party and we're invited.

MARTIN Orr, the party's finished!

PENNY What do you mean?

WILLIE No it hasn't, he's fibbing!

MARTIN Yeah it has ... hasn't it? *(He kicks Michael.)*

MICHAEL Oh yeah, it has! I know ... 'cos he's kicking me!

MARTIN It was on this afternoon and they ate piles of food but all the kids have gone home now and you're too late!

VAL Oh, we *haven't* missed it, have we?

PENNY You said you rang Melanie up!

WILLIE I did! I ranged her up on the telephone this afternoon! And the party wasn't on then, so tell him he's lying.

PENNY You're lying.

MARTIN No I'm not lying.

WILLIE He is! Tell him he is!

PENNY You are.

MARTIN No I'm not, am I?

MICHAEL No he's not. You've missed it!

WILLIE No we haven't ... Look ... It's not that gate there, 'cos them kids came out of that one ... and it's not that gate, 'cos they live there ... I bet it's that one!

(WILLIE runs across to Melanie's gate. MARTIN and MICHAEL run in front of him.)

WILLIE It is! Look! It's this one! Let me through!

(PENNY and VAL whisper together on the far side of the stage. They link arms, and while WILLIE argues with MARTIN and MICHAEL, they skip across, chanting.)

VAL, PENNY Any-body in the way gets a big *kick*!

(VAL and PENNY kick MARTIN. He clutches his leg in pain. Val, Penny and Willie fall about laughing.)

WILLIE Yarr! He's going to start crying now! Big baby!

PENNY That sorted you out, didn't it?

MARTIN No, it din't I'm off to get some more kids!

(MARTIN suddenly runs off down the alley.)

MICHAEL Martin! *Martin*! Come back! Orr, no!

WILLIE Ah, you're on your own now! What are you going to do? You can't stop us going in now.

PENNY Do you want us to kick *you* as well? 'Cos I can kick really hard!

VAL So can I!

WILLIE Yeah, they can ... an they'll make your cry!

MICHAEL Orr no, err, anyway ... I've got to go in for a baba!

(Michael runs to his gate, clutching his bum.)

PENNY *(Running after him)* Oh, can I come and watch?

(MICHAEL tries to close the gate but Penny forces her way through. She closes the gate and bolts it after them.)

MICHAEL No!!

PENNY Go on! Let me!

MICHAEL No! Gerrout!

WILLIE Penny! Penny!

(WILLIE runs over and knocks on the gate.)

WILLIE *Penny*!! Orr, what's she doing? She's gone in there are she's left me out here and we're supposed to be going to a party, not hanging round a mucky ten-foot. I *hate* it ... !

VAL Be quiet! She'll have to come out soon. Let's knock on the gate and call together.

(VAL and WILLIE start knocking on the gate and calling PENNY. As they get louder BRIAN enters again. He stands behind them, joining in the calling and jumping up and down. Willie and Val gradually realise he is there. They stop shouting, leaving Brian shouting alone.)

BRIAN Penny! Penny! Pe-nny! Pen ...

WILLIE Who are you?

BRIAN Superboy!

VAL You look more like Super-Rat!

WILLIE What do you want?

BRIAN Do you want to play with me?

VAL Err no! We don't play with little rats, do we?

WILLIE *(Whispering to Val)* Hey, listen!

VAL Alright, we'll play with you then.

BRIAN Orr, great! I know a great game ...

(WILLIE and VAL grab BRIAN by his arms and walk him downstage.)

WILLIE We know a great game as well ... We'll play at ... throwing you over that wall into the graveyard!

(They lift him up.)

BRIAN No! Let go!

WILLIE Right! After three. Ready? One ... Two ...

(MARTIN returns with JENNY.)

MARTIN *Hey*! Hey, Brian! Yer mam says you've got to go in for your tea.

BRIAN I've had me tea, clever clogs!

MARTIN She says you haven't had enough. You've got to go in for some more!

WILLIE Yeah, go on home, rat!

(BRIAN leaves to jeers from WILLIE and VAL.)

JENNY Is that the lass?

MARTIN No.

JENNY Good! I'll go home for me tea now ...

MARTIN Hang on ... Where's she gone? Where's our Michael?

WILLIE They've gone in there together and they've locked the gate and she's watching him ...

VAL Don't tell him what they're doing!

WILLIE Well, they're doing something and it's not very nice and she shouldn't be in there and ...

(MARTIN bangs on the gate and shouts 'Michael'. The others join in. The gate opens and PENNY and MICHAEL come out.)

PENNY *Guess* what I've seen!

JENNY What?

PENNY I've seen his ferret!

WILLIE What colour is it?

PENNY Blue!

WILLIE Don't be stupid! You don't get blue ferrets!

MARTIN Have you been showing her our ferret?

MICHAEL She just saw it on accident!

PENNY No I never! You showed me it on purpose! You said, 'You can't see me baba but you can see me ferret instead if you like.'

MICHAEL I didn't!

PENNY Yes he did!

WILLIE I'm fed up of this! I want to go to Melanie's party and I'm going to go now and you'd better come as well!

(WILLIE stomps over to Melanie's gate and knocks loudly.)

PENNY Willie gets ever so annoyed sometimes.

MICHAEL He's got a big mouth, 'asn't he?

PENNY Yeah.

(MELANIE opens her gate.)

MELANIE Hello, Willie.

WILLIE Hello, Melanie. I've got you a Rupert jigsaw for your birthday and I bought it with my own money. Happy birthday!

MELANIE Oh, thank you. Come in then – the party's just starting and we're going to eat now ... Are Penny and Valerie coming?

WILLIE *Penny*! Melanie says you've got to come in to the party *now*, 'cos they're starting the food now. And you, Valerie.

PENNY Orr, alright. Tara, then ... I'll see your ferret again sometime.

WILLIE No you won't! Come on!

(PENNY and VAL also wish MELANIE 'happy birthday' and give her presents. They all exit into Melanie's.)

JENNY I'm bored!

MICHAEL I want a baba!

JENNY *(Starting to leave)* I've got to go in for my tea now.

MARTIN Right, see you then, Jenny!

(ANGELA and NICOLA arrive. Nicola is crying. They meet JENNY leaving.)

JENNY What's up?

ANGELA We're looking for Melanie's back gate and we're late for her party and she's crying ...

JENNY *Martin*!! Show these lasses where Melanie's is! Tara!

(JENNY goes off.)

ANGELA 'Bye 'bye. Thank you!

(To Nicola) Come on and stop crying ... we'll find it now!

(ANGELA and NICOLA cross to MICHAEL and MARTIN. Nicola sniffles.)

ANGELA Can you show us where Melanie's is, please?

NICOLA We've come for a party!

MICHAEL Well, we don't know and we don't care, 'cos I'm going in for a baba ... and you *can't come and watch!*

(NICOLA bursts into floods of tears and howling. MICHAEL exits and bolts his gate.)

ANGELA That wasn't very nice! She's crying again now!

MARTIN Orr, no! Sshh! Don't cry! Ssshhh! Somebody might think I've hit you!! Sssshhhh! Stop it! Hey ... ! Hey ... ! Do you want to see my ferret?

(There is a moment of silence. Then NICOLA bursts out howling even louder. MARTIN crosses to Melanie's gate and knocks. It is opened by MELANIE.)

MARTIN Hello, Melanie, there's some lasses for you ... but she's crying.

MELANIE Hello! What's the matter, Nicola?

ANGELA *He* made her cry!

MARTIN I didn't!

ANGELA Happy birthday, Melanie. Many happy returns.

MELANIE Thank you. Hurry up and go in because we thought you weren't coming and we've started the food now.

NICOLA Happy birthday, Melanie.

MELANIE Thank you.

(ANGELA and NICOLA go in. MELANIE lingers at the gate. MARTIN steps forward.)

MELANIE Did you hit my friend?

MARTIN No! Honestly, I didn't!

MELANIE Because it wouldn't be very nice if you did. I wouldn't like you.

MARTIN No! I don't hit girls! Honest! *(Trying to change the subject)* Hey! Hey ... what's your party like? Is it good?

MELANIE Yes, it's lovely!

MARTIN Are you going to play games after?

MELANIE Yes! We're going to play pass-the-parcel ...

MELANIE'S MUM *(Off-stage)* Melanie! Close that gate at once!

MELANIE I'll have to go now.

MARTIN Yeah ... Did you get many presents? I'd have given you a nice present ... if I'd been invited ...

MELANIE'S MUM *(Off-stage)* I won't tell you again!

MELANIE Well ... 'Bye 'bye, Martin.

MARTIN 'Bye 'bye, Melanie ... I might see you after!

MELANIE Yes ... 'Bye 'bye!

(MELANIE goes. The gate closes. MARTIN stands looking at it.)

MELANIE'S MUM *(Off-stage)* Who *were* you talking to? I've *told* you about that before!

(We hear a smack off-stage and MELANIE bursts into tears. MARTIN looks miserable. His gate opens. MICHAEL appears, looking happier.)

MICHAEL Hey! Was you talking nice to Smellanie?

MARTIN No, I wasn't!

MICHAEL Well, what did her mam hit her for then?

MARTIN I dunno, do I?

MICHAEL Orr, you wanna see her party though! They've got tons of sandwiches *that* thick, 'cos they've got so many different sorts of things in 'em and *loads* of cream cakes and fruit and jelly and *piles* of little buns with icing and coloured bits on and everything ... and they're having ice-cream and things after and she's got a birthday cake as well. Oh, and they've got apple-pie as well!!

MARTIN Oorr ... ! I'm starving – aren't you?

MICHAEL Orr, yeah! Mam says you've got to come in for your tea now.

MARTIN Oh good! What we having?

MICHAEL *(His expression changing dramatically)* Pilchards on toast!

MARTIN Orr, no! Not pilchards! She *knows* I hate pilchards!

(MICHAEL and MARTIN start to leave.)

MICHAEL I know! I think she does it out of badness!

(They close the gate behind them.)

MICHAEL Hey! I've had this *great* idea what we can do after tea, though ...

End of Act One

ACT TWO

AFTER TEA

We hear small voices from Melanie's garden, slightly out of tune, singing, 'happy birthday, dear Melanie'. This is followed by, 'three cheers for Melanie – hip-pip!' etc. BRIAN appears on his BMX bike, with his siren going. He stops, dismounts. He glances at Melanie's, then crosses to Shane's gate and knocks.

BRIAN Sha-ane! Shane! Are you coming out?

(There is a silence – then a crash comes from Michael's followed by whispered voices.)

MARTIN *(Off-stage)* Ssshhh!

MICHAEL Sorry!

(BRIAN goes over and knocks on MICHAEL and MARTIN's gate.)

BRIAN Michael! It's Brian! Are you coming out ... 'Ey? Go on ...! I know you're there ... Are you coming out?

(MARTIN's head appears over the fence.)

MARTIN Hey! What do you want?

BRIAN Is your Michael coming out to play?

MARTIN No, he can't – he's busy.

BRIAN What's he doing?

MARTIN We're making summat.

BRIAN What y' making?

MARTIN It's a secret. I can't tell you.

BRIAN Go on! I won't tell anybody.

MARTIN No! It's a secret! I can't tell you a secret. Go on, go and play up your own end!

BRIAN No! There's nobody up there and I've got nothin' to do up there!

MARTIN *(Pointing)* Hey! Look at that helicopter!

(BRIAN turns round. MARTIN disappears behind the fence.)

BRIAN Where? *(He turns back.)* Orr, yer a liar, ...

(BRIAN picks up his bike and rides off, cursing. MICHAEL's head appears over his fence.)

MICHAEL It's alright, Martin ... he's gone.

(The gate opens. MARTIN appears carrying a crudely painted sign saying 'Beware of the Ferrit.' MICHAEL follows him out.)

MICHAEL Hang it on that nail there!

MARTIN *(Hanging the sign on the fence)* Orr, yeah – that's really great, that!

MICHAEL *(Admiring the sign)* Yeah, that'll really frighten 'em, that!

MARTIN They won't come near our gate again.

(MICHAEL and MARTIN go in again and close their gate. The stage is empty. Melanie's gate opens. PENNY appears, dragging GEORGE after her.)

PENNY Quick, George, she's not looking. We can play out here!

GEORGE Orr ... we can't do it here! Somebody might come and see us!

PENNY No they won't

(MICHAEL's head pops up above his fence and shoots down again.)

MICHAEL Hey, Martin! It's that kid what hit me.

GEORGE Hey, I heard something ... there's somebody listening!

PENNY No there isn't.

(MARTIN opens the gate and comes out, carrying the hammer.)

MARTIN Hey! What you doing out here?

GEORGE We're gonna play rudies! D'you wanna play?

MARTIN Errr ...

GEORGE Hey, what you doing with that hammer? I bet you put that daft sign up, didn't you? Thicko! You don't spell 'ferret' like that!

(MICHAEL has followed MARTIN out.)

MICHAEL Well, that dun't matter anyway, 'cos we've built a secret den!

MARTIN Shurrup! It's supposed to be a secret!

PENNY Secret den!?

GEORGE Hey!

PENNY Can we have a look at it?

GEORGE Hey, we could play rudies in it!

PENNY Oh yeah!

MICHAEL How do you play rudies?

GEORGE }
PENNY } Don't y' know?

GEORGE I'll tell you!

(GEORGE leans over and whispers to MICHAEL. At first he looks worried then very interested. He whispers to MARTIN, along with suitable gestures. As he does so, KEITH, JOHN and NIGEL run on from down the alley.)

GEORGE Hey, kids! Do you want to play *rudies* with us? We're going in their secret den!

KEITH, JOHN, NIGEL Yeah!!

KEITH How d'you play rudies?

MICHAEL Don't y' know?

PENNY I'll show you! Come on.

(PENNY goes through MICHAEL's gate. George and all the others follow.)

MARTIN Hey no! It's not all that big!

MICHAEL Don't be a spoilsport!

MARTIN They won't all fit in!

MICHAEL Can I go first ... ?

(MARTIN follows the others in and closes the gate. We hear giggles, then off-stage the sound of Brian's siren. BRIAN appears on his BMX bike. He dismounts, looks round, listens and crosses to Michael's gate. He knocks.)

BRIAN Michael! Are you coming out to play? *(Muffled giggles)* I know y' there, 'cos I can hear you! It's Brian again ... Are you coming out? *(He knocks again – silence.)* Hey, Michael, I like your sign ...! I can't read it though ... Are you coming out or not ... ? I'm waiting for an answer! Right! I'm sitting right down here till you come out ... and I mean it!

(BRIAN sits down against the fence, under the 'Beware of the Ferrit' sign. JENNY and ROBYN enter from right, chatting. They stop when they see Brian.)

JENNY It's Brian, look.

ROBYN No! No! It's a ferret! *(They screech with laughter.)*

JENNY Yeeurgh! A smelly ferret!

BRIAN I'm not a ferret, stupid!

ROBYN I wonder if it bites? Does the little ferret bite?

BRIAN Leave me alone! I'm not a ferret ... and I'm getting me trousers mucky down here!

JENNY You need new ones anyway.

BRIAN You shurrup! Me mam says I can have some new ones when these get worn out properly!

ROBYN The ferret's got dicks as well!

BRIAN Gerroff! And I haven't got dicks though! My teacher says I *'aven't* got dicks!

JENNY He's even got a nose like a ferret!

ROBYN Ferret! ferret! ferret!

BRIAN Right I'm fed up!! *(He runs to his bike.)* I'm gonna get you into trouble now! And I mean it this time! I'm getting a policeman!

(BRIAN **hurtles off down the alley.)**

JENNY }
ROBYN } Ferret! ferret! ferret! ferret! ferret! ... !

JENNY Orr, Robyn, what if he does get a policeman? We might get into trouble!

ROBYN He won't ... *(Giggling)* Ferrets can't talk!

JENNY It's not funny any more, Robyn! We might get into trouble!

(Melanie's gate opens. WILLIE **appears, looking for** PENNY.**)**

WILLIE Hiya!

JENNY Oh, hiya, thingy!

ROBYN Who's that?

WILLIE I'm Willie.

ROBYN I'm Robyn.

WILLIE Hiya!

ROBYN Hiya!

WILLIE Are you a boy?

ROBYN Are you a girl?

JENNY What are you doing out on this ten-foot anyway? I thought you was at Melanie's party.

WILLIE I'm looking for my sister, Penny. Have you seen her?

JENNY No.

WILLIE Well she's out here somewhere ... and so is George!

JENNY Orr, I bet I know where she is. She went in Michael's before, din't she – to watch him have a baba! I bet they've gone in there!

WILLIE D'you think she's in there again with him now?

JENNY Yeah.

WILLIE God, he goes to baba a lot, doesn't he?

ROBYN I'll show you how to get them out!

(ROBYN hammers on the gate. They see who can shout 'Penny' the loudest.)

WILLIE Penny! Melanie's mum says you've got to come back to the party now or you can't come back at all...! I know you're in there. I'll tell mum you've been naughty again if you don't come *now*!

(The gate opens. PENNY appears, looking very naughty. She is followed by GEORGE, MICHAEL, MARTIN, KEITH, JOHN and NIGEL. They look very furtive. Nobody says anything for a while.)

WILLIE What *have* you been doing in there?

PENNY Playing!

WILLIE Playing what though?

PENNY Just playing! *(Some of the boys snigger.)*

JENNY There's you're brother there, look!

(ROBYN barges through and drags NIGEL out by the ear.)

ROBYN Hey! Was you in there?

NIGEL Yeah.

(ROBYN smacks NIGEL round the head.)

ROBYN Clear off home! I'm gonna tell me mam of you!

NIGEL *(Starting to leave)* Alright! I'm going!

GEORGE Hey, kid! It was worth getting smacked round the head for, though, wasn't it?

(All the boys laugh. NIGEL goes off. MELANIE appears at her gate.)

MELANIE My mummy says if you don't come back in *now* you've got to stay out here! We're playing games now!!

MICHAEL Hey, are you playing 'rudies'?

MELANIE No!

(The boys start giggling again.)

WILLIE We're coming in now, Melanie. Come on, you! We're going back into Melanie's to play *nice* games!

(WILLIE drags PENNY across to Melanie's.)

PENNY Are you coming, George?

GEORGE No. I'm staying out here to play with this lot.

WILLIE Good! Come on, you!

(WILLIE drags PENNY through the gate.)

PENNY 'Bye, everybody!

(Very friendly 'byes' from all the boys. PENNY **and** WILLIE **exit.)**

MARTIN Hey, George, what's Melanie's party like?

GEORGE Orr, it was ace! There was *tons* to eat and drink! I didn't fancy the games they was going to play, though – they were a bit soft! *(Pause)* Hey, I tell you what, we could play really good game out here though! D'you wanna? *(Cries of 'yeah!' etc.)* Let's play 'tig'!

(BRIAN **enters on his bike.)**

ROBYN Oh no, look! It's ferret-features again.

JENNY I thought you were going to see a policeman!

BRIAN I did! And he said he'll let you off this time but you've all got to let me play with you.

ROBYN Liar! You haven't seen a policeman at all!

JENNY Who wants to play with you, anyway?

GEORGE Hey, no, that's alright! He can be 'it' for tig!

ALL Yeah!

GEORGE C'mon little squirt, you've got to try and tig somebody!

(GEORGE **smacks** BRIAN **and runs away. So do all the others, jeering. Brian tries desperately to touch someone but is easily outpaced. He stops.**

BRIAN That's not fair! You're all running faster than me!

MICHAEL That's 'cos we're faster than you!

MARTIN Don't they even teach you to run at your school?

BRIAN 'Course they do!

KEITH *(To John)* He doesn't even go to the same school as the rest of us.

JOHN Neither do I.

KEITH Yeah, but you're not from round here, are you?

BRIAN It's not my fault!

GEORGE What school do you go to, kid?

BRIAN St Peter's

GEORGE Err, that's for thickos, isn't it?

ALL Yeah!

BRIAN No it's not! I have to go there 'cos of the church ... so there!

ROBYN Do you go to church then?

BRIAN No.

ROBYN Well then, that proves you're thick!

ALL *(Jeering and laughing)* Yeah!

GEORGE Hey, no, look ... he can't help it. Tell you what, I'll be 'it' instead and give you a chance. OK, squirt?

BRIAN Yeah, OK.

GEORGE Right. Ready, go!

(GEORGE runs and smacks BRIAN's head.)

GEORGE You're 'it' again!

BRIAN *(Close to tears)* That's not fair ... you didn't give me a chance!

JENNY You shouldn't be so slow, should you?

MICHAEL Hey, I've got an idea! Everybody come here ...

(They all gather in a huddle, leaving BRIAN on one side. Hurried whispers and giggles. Brian looks worried. They break apart.)

MARTIN Right! We're going to give you a real chance this time ... we'll have a girl as 'it'.

JENNY Yeah, I'll be on ... and I won't try and tig you first, Brian. OK?

BRIAN *(Still looking worried)* Alright then.

JENNY Right ... Go!

(JENNY moves away from BRIAN, pretending to try to touch the others, who stay out of her reach. Brian stands still. Meanwhile, MICHAEL works his way behind Brian and kneels down.)

MARTIN Now!

(JENNY suddenly runs for BRIAN who turns to run away, trips over MICHAEL and falls flat. Everybody bursts out laughing. Brian stays on the floor, writhing in 'pain' and crying.)

ROBYN Yerr, look ... ferret-face is crying again!

(ROBYN pokes BRIAN with her foot.)

BRIAN Leave me alone!

GEORGE He's only putting it on ... great snotty cry-baby!

(GEORGE kicks BRIAN. Brian leaps up, blind with anger and frustration.)

BRIAN I'm not! I'm gonna kill you!

(BRIAN tries desperately to attack GEORGE who easily holds him off while the others laugh. George finally shoves him back. MARTIN sticks his leg out and trips him up. Brian falls onto his backside and sits there sobbing, as the others all laugh and jeer.)

MICHAEL Why don't you run home to your mam, then, as usual?

ROBYN Yeah, go to your mam ... she smells as well!

(BRIAN stands up, but he is completely defeated now.)

BRIAN No she doesn't then! I'm going to tell her what you said!

MARTIN Yeah, she'll probably start crying as well! *(They all laugh.)*

BRIAN I'm going ... and I'm *never* coming back this time! *(He starts to go.)*

JENNY Good! I hope we never see you again!

GEORGE *(Picking up Brian's BMX)* Here, squirt, don't forget your crappy bike.

BRIAN Gerroff it!

(BRIAN snatches his bike away and wheels it off, sniffing. The others shout after him. Brian jumps on the bike and rides away.)

JENNY And don't come back!

(The jeering dies out. There is a pause.)

KEITH What we gonna do now?

GEORGE Hey! Do you know how to play Stick-in-the-Mud?

ROBYN Oh yeah, I know how to play that! One person's on and if they tig you, you have to stand still but with your legs open ...

GEORGE And if anybody else crawls through your legs you're free again! OK ... Right, I'll be on first then. Go!

(The game begins. As GEORGE 'tigs' people, they stand still with legs apart. Some are freed by others crawling through their legs. Everyone is having great fun. JENNY is tigged near the front of the acting area.)

JENNY *Help*! I'm stuck! Somebody get us out!

(While the game continues, KEITH manages to crawl through JENNY's legs but gets stuck with his head up her skirt. Jenny screams very loudly. They all stop.)

JENNY You look up my skirt an' I'll ... wee-wee on your head!

GEORGE Yaarrgh, you mucky sod!

(They all laugh and tease KEITH, who gets very embarrassed.)

GEORGE Hey, this game's boring now ... let's do something else. I know! Let's play 'Chainies' ... that's where when you're tigged you have to hold hands to tig the others, so its ends up with a big chain ... And you can be on first *(indicating John)* 'cos you've got a daft voice!

(They all run away. As JOHN tigs them one by one, they join hands until only MICHAEL remains free.)

MICHAEL Ha! You 'aven't got me yet!

(The chain suddenly surrounds MICHAEL. They close in.)

GEORGE All pile on!

(MICHAEL is shoved to the ground and everybody dives on top in a pile.)

MICHAEL *Gerroff* ...! Gerroff! ... or I'm gonna *poo*!

(They all equally rapidly pile off.

By now the amber light of the street-lamp in the centre has come on and fades up over the next few minutes. The daylight has begun to dwindle and gradually disappears by the end of the play.

As the kids clamber off MICHAEL, we hear the sound of a police siren – faint at first, it becomes very loud, then fades slightly and stops.)

GEORGE Hey! What was that? It's stopped near the top of your street!

(Immediately a second siren is heard, just like the first.)

GEORGE Hey! There's another one! It might be a big fire!

MARTIN C'mon! Let's go and look!

GEORGE Yeah, I'll race y' there! Come on!

(All the boys rush off down the alley in excitement. ROBYN grabs JENNY's hand and starts to follow. Jenny resists.)

ROBYN Come on, Jenny!

JENNY I don't want to go!

ROBYN Orr! Why not?

JENNY 'Cos me mam says I've not got to go off the ten-foot after me tea ... and anyway, it's starting to get dark now and I'll have to go in soon!

ROBYN Well, I can go up there.

JENNY Well, your mam's different to my mam!

ROBYN Orr ... well what we gonna do now then?

JENNY I dunno. ...!

(They lapse into contemplation of this eternal question, still holding hands. There is a pause. Melanie's gate opens. MAGGIE **and** SAM **appear, followed by** MELANIE. **They are saying goodbye.)**

MAGGIE Thanks for a nice party, Melanie ... it was smashing!

SAM Yes, happy birthday! And we'll see you on Monday at dance class.

MELANIE Yes, alright. I'm sorry you've got to go. Thank you for coming ... 'Bye then.

(MELANIE **disappears. The gate closes. They cross to** JENNY **and** ROBYN.**)**

MAGGIE Excuse me, have you seen our brother George?

ROBYN Oh yeah, did you hear that siren? Well, he ran off after it with all the other kids, and we were going to go as well ... only *she* wouldn't – but I would!

JENNY It's not *my* fault!

SAM Well, George shouldn't have gone anyway!

MAGGIE Right! I'm going to tell my mum of him, 'cos she told him he had to take us home, didn't she?

SAM He never does as he's told, our George.

JENNY He's got a big mouth as well, hasn't he?

MAGGIE Yeah!

ROBYN Anyway, you can stay here with us until he gets back.

MAGGIE Alright then ... Do you want a sausage-roll? *(She produces one.)*

ROBYN I don't eat sausage-rolls.

JENNY I do! *(She takes it.)* It's all broken!

MAGGIE Well, it's been in my pocket. Hey, I've got a sandwich in my tights!

JENNY Yeeurgh!

ROBYN What sort is it?

MAGGIE Peanut butter.

ROBYN Great, Can I have it? *(She takes it and eats it.)*

JENNY Yeeurgh! Robyn!

ROBYN Have you got any jelly?

SAM Don't be daft! Where could we put jelly?

(JENNY quickly whispers something to ROBYN, they both burst out laughing.

MAGGIE What you laughing at?

(GEORGE suddenly runs back on.)

GEORGE Hiya, snotbags!

MAGGIE You shurrup, you! Where've you been?

ROBYN Hey, what was it, down the street?

GEORGE Orr, there's been an accident on the road and there was police cars and an ambulance and everything ...

ROBYN Oh! We'll have missed it all now! *You*!!

JENNY *(Changing the subject)* Hey! George ... you know everybody at that party of Melanie's goes dancing, don't they? Do you go?

GEORGE Err ... Orr no, I don't go!

SAM }
MAGGIE } Oh yes you do!

ROBYN Yarr! You big sissy! *I* go to judo!

GEORGE Well *I* go to karate! *(He chops the air viciously.)*

SAM }
MAGGIE } Oh no you don't!

GEORGE Well I only go to dancing because my mum makes me ... the old cow!

SAM Ohh! I'm going to tell her what you said!

GEORGE I don't care.

JENNY Well, I'm going to start going to dancing as well, anyway.

ROBYN Hey! You could start coming to my judo class with me if you wanted.

GEORGE Oh, that'd be great!

MAGGIE Anyway, George, look ... it's starting to get dark now. We'll have to be going home or we'll all get into trouble.

GEORGE Yeah, alright then.

JENNY Well, why don't you all come round and play with us round here tomorrow? Do you want to?

SAM Shall we, Maggie? We can come in our playing-out clothes tomorrow.

MAGGIE Alright then ... and if we ask our mum we might be able to bring our dance shoes and costumes to show you.

JENNY Orr, great!

ROBYN Are you coming as well, George? And I'll show you my judo suit.

GEORGE Yeah! Right!

ROBYN And I can show you how to do throwing people and strangling ...

SAM And we can show you some more dancing.

JENNY Oh, that'll be really good. We'll have a really good time!

MAGGIE Come on then, George, we'll have to go now.

(MAGGIE and SAM start to leave)

ROBYN Come real early then, and if we're not out just wait for u ... or, I live at number 17 and she lives at number 33 and just knock on our door.

GEORGE Yeah, alright. See you tomorrow then.

SAM Hurry up, George! We'll see you in the morning then. 'Bye!

(They all say 'bye'. MAGGIE, SAM and GEORGE exit.)

JENNY Oh, that'll be really good fun tomorrow, won't it?

ROBYN Yeah!

(Melanie's gate opens as they talk. WILLIE emerges, followed by PENNY, VAL and MELANIE.)

WILLIE 'Bye 'bye, Melanie.

PENNY 'Bye, Melanie. Thanks for a lovely party.

VAL 'Bye. See you on Monday, Melanie.

WILLIE Yes, and tell your mum sorry ... for everything!

(They turn to go. MELANIE lingers at the gate.)

ROBYN Hey! Hiya!

WILLIE Hiya *(They all say hello.)*

JENNY Was Melanie's party really good?

WILLIE Yes it was. We had jelly and ice-cream and everything . and Angela and Nicola had to leave early 'cos Nicola w sick ... and we were the last to leave, weren't we?

PENNY Yes, the very very last.

WILLIE Yes, but I did have to help Melanie's mum to clean the dog cacca off the carpet, though!

VAL She wasn't very pleased with you, was she?

WILLIE No, especially when I was showing her how to do my new dance and I kicked the limeade all over the place.

JENNY Hey! Do you go dancing as well, then?

ROBYN Does your mam make you go?

WILLIE No, I like to go!

JENNY Well, do you know what? I'm going to start going as well. I'm going with George's sisters.

ROBYN Hey, yeah, and do you know what else? George and his sisters are coming round here to play tomorrow.

PENNY Are they? Is George coming round? I *like* George!

WILLIE I don't! He's rude! And he's a big gob!

ROBYN No he's not! He's good is George.

PENNY What's he coming round here for?

JENNY 'Cos we asked him to. We'll ask you as well, if you want.

ROBYN Yeah, do you want to come and play as well?

VAL Can we?

JENNY 'Course you can. It'll be really good fun if everybody comes.

ROBYN Are you coming then?

PENNY Yes we are, aren't we, Willie?

WILLIE I suppose so. Are you coming, Valerie?

VAL Ooh Yes!

WILLIE Alright then, we'll see you tomorrow ... but we'll have to go now or we won't be allowed out.

PENNY Yeah, we're supposed to be in before dark.

WILLIE Come on, you!

(WILLIE drags PENNY off. VAL follows. ROBYN shouts after them.)

ROBYN Well I live at number 17 and she lives at number 33, so just knock on our door if we're not out or just wait for us ... George and them are coming real early!

PENNY Alright ... see you in the morning! 'Bye!

(WILLIE, PENNY and VAL exit. JENNY and ROBYN walk back. MELANIE is still at her gate.)

JENNY There's Melanie over there, look.

ROBYN Yeah, she's all by herself.

JENNY Let's go and talk to her.

ROBYN No, she stinks

JENNY No she doesn't! Come on ... *(Crossing over)* Hiya, Melanie

MELANIE Hello.

JENNY Did you have a nice party?

BRIAN Yes, thank you.

JENNY What presents did you get from the other kids?

MELANIE I got a Rupert jigsaw and some chocolates and books .. and a dolly that drinks from a bottle and ...

ROBYN Hey! Guess what! George and his sisters are coming round to play with us tomorrow

MELANIE *(Looking quite sad)* Are Willie and Penny and Valerie com ing as well?

ROBYN Yeah, they're all coming!

JENNY Why don't you come out and play with us as well, Melanie? You never come out and play with us.

MELANIE Can I? *(Excited)* Can I come and play with you?

JENNY 'Course you can! You can show us all the games you played at your party.

ROBYN Yeah, we heard lots of screaming and laughing ... you didn't invite us though, did you?

MELANIE Well ... I would have done ... but my mummy wouldn't let me.

JENNY See! It's not her fault ... you know what her mam's like! Will she let you come out to play then?

MELANIE Well, I'll ask her.

ROBYN You could say it'd be a treat for your birthday!

MELANIE I'll try really hard! I'll ask my dad as well, because he's really nice ... if he's not too tired.

JENNY What does he do, your dad?

MELANIE'S MUM *(Off-stage)* Come on, Melanie! Bedtime! You've had a very busy day ...

MELANIE Oh, I'll have to go in now. I'll try and come out tomorrow, though.

ROBYN Tell her all your friends are coming to play as well!

MELANIE Alright. I might see you tomorrow then.

MELANIE'S MUM *(Off-stage)* Melanie! Did you hear me? Come along!

JENNY See you, then.

MELANIE I hope so! 'Bye!

(MELANIE **hurries away.)**

ROBYN I s'pose she'd be alright, Melanie, if it wasn't for her mam!

JENNY Yeah, well, y' can't help having a mam, can you?

ROBYN No, it's funny, isn't it?

JENNY Mmmn ...

(As ROBYN and JENNY lapse into a thoughtful and slightly puzzled silence over this CHARLIE enters with SHANE still in his cub uniform. Shane is crying and has a grazed knee.)

SHANE I want me mam!

ROBYN Hey, are you just coming back from cubs? You're late! What have you been doing?

SHANE She lost the key!

CHARLIE No I didn't! We were just coming back from cubs and then we found we hadn't got the key and we went all the way back to look for it and then he fell down and cut his knee and we still didn't find it ... and you can just go on your own next time! I'm telling me mam I'm not taking you any more!

(ROBYN has gone over to SHANE and tries to touch his bleeding knee.)

ROBYN Yeeurgh!

SHANE Gerroff! Don't touch it! I might bleed to death!

CHARLIE Orr, what we gonna do?

JENNY Why don't you go round the front and knock on your front door for your mam to let you in and then you can come and let Shane in the back.

ROBYN Yeah, and I'll look after your brother for you! *(She grabs Shane.)*

SHANE No! Don't leave me with them! Don't leave me with them!

CHARLIE Alright, I won't be long. I'll come and open the gate.

(CHARLIE exits.)

SHANE No! Don't pull me woggle! Don't pull me woggle!!

ROBYN I'm not touching your woggle ... y' big cry-baby!

JENNY Hey, guess who's coming round to play tomorrow, Shane.

SHANE I don't know and I don't care!

ROBYN George is coming round.

JENNY And his sisters ... and Penny and all them other kids from Melanie's party.

ROBYN And Melanie might come out to play as well.

SHANE I don't care!

SHANE'S MUM *(Off-stage)* Shane! Charlotte! Are you out there? Come on! You should have been in ages ago!

SHANE Oh no! It's me mam. She might not let me go to cubs any more now!

ROBYN Hey, I've got a great idea how you can get in – you can crawl under your gate!

JENNY Yeah!

SHANE Oh no, it's too small. I won't fit!

ROBYN 'Course you will. Come on!

JENNY We'll help you!

(ROBYN **and** JENNY **grab** SHANE **and shove him under the gate. Feet first.)**

SHANE No! Gerroff me ... ! Oh no! I'm *stuck* now!

ROBYN No you're not. You breathe in and we'll shove you through. Right ... push!

SHANE No, I can't! Stop it!

(We hear CHARLIE**'s voice from the other side of the gate.)**

CHARLIE Shane! What you doing under there, stupid?

SHANE I'm stuck!

CHARLIE Mam's ever so upset. She heard an ambulance and she thought you might have been run over!

SHANE It's not my fault! Open the gate.

CHARLIE I can't open the gate with you stuck there, can I?

JENNY Charlotte! You grab his legs and pull and we'll shove!

CHARLIE Alright.

SHANE No! Stop it! You're stretching me! Stop!

ROBYN Shurrup, Shane! Charlie! Tell you what ... you push instead and we'll pull.

(ROBYN and JENNY grab SHANE's arms and pull.)

SHANE Give up! Yaargh!

(The girls succeed in pulling SHANE out. The gate opens. CHARLIE appears.)

CHARLIE You stupid idiot!

SHANE It wasn't my fault. They made me!

ROBYN No we didn't. Don't lie!

(SHANE is on his knees, crying.)

SHANE Why do 'orrible things always happen to me? I had to take her baby's knickers off and it didn't have a bum, and *she* bust my bow and arrow. We lost the key and I've cut me knee ...

JENNY Hey, he's a poet!

(Their laughter makes SHANE even more upset.)

SHANE And then I get jammed under our gate and ... and last night I nearly flippin' drowned in the bath!

CHARLIE He always gets like this when it's past his bedtime!

SHANE No I don't! It's not past me bedtime anyway!

CHARLIE Yes it is, then! And I'm gonna go in and tell me mam how *you* lost the key and you're gonna be in *big* trouble!

(CHARLIE exits. Leaving SHANE crying.)

JENNY Cry-baby bunting.

ROBYN Yer daddy's gone a hunting ...

(MARTIN and MICHAEL run on from the alley.)

MARTIN Hey! Hey! There's been a road accident!

ROBYN We *know*! George told us. Ner!

JENNY Yeah, and guess what? George is coming round to play tomorrow with his sisters and *Penny* and all them other kids and ...

MICHAEL Yeah but *listen*! A kid's been run over and somebody said it might be *Brian Sullivan*!

MARTIN And he might be *dead*!

(JENNY is stunned into silence.)

ROBYN Did ... did you see him?

MARTIN No, the ambulance had taken him away when we got there ... and there was this BMX bike all crumpled up in the gutter ...

MICHAEL And there was blood all over the road!

(JENNY wanders off to one side, starting to cry.)

SHANE Brian was always riding his bike on the main road, wasn't he? And he didn't even have any lights on it, either!

MICHAEL He should have stayed in the ten-foot where it was safe.

MARTIN Yeah, but ... nobody'd play with him would they?

(JENNY sniffs and chokes. There is silence, then CHARLIE reappears.)

CHARLIE Shane! You get in *now*. Mam's ever so mad with you!

SHANE Oh no! Now I'm in for it! It's all your fault! I'm telling her it was your fault, anyway!

(SHANE runs in. JENNY is now crying quite openly. The others are trying not to. CHARLIE crosses to Jenny.)

CHARLIE What's a matter, Jenny?

JENNY Well ... It wasn't our fault, but ... *(She chokes up.)*

CHARLIE What? What's up?

JENNY Brian Sullivan's *dead*!

CHARLIE He's not!

JENNY He is! And ... and, well, we started teasing him when he was sat under the ferret sign outside their gate, calling him ferret-face and horrible things like that ... and then when he came back, we hurt him and he ran off crying and I said ... I said ... I hope we never see you again ... and now he's *dead* ... and I'm a murderer! And it's all my fault!

(JENNY runs off, crying helplessly. ROBYN starts to follow.)

ROBYN Oh no, Jenny, don't go in crying!

JENNY Leave me alone!

(JENNY exits. There is more silence, then ROBYN turns back to the others.)

ROBYN It's all your fault and that stupid sign! If you hadn't put it up he might still be alive!

(ROBYN suddenly rips down the 'Beware of the Ferrit' sign from the gate, throws it to the ground and runs off the other way, starting to cry.)

CHARLIE Orr ... I'd better go in and tell me mam ... I'll see you.

(CHARLIE dashes in, on the verge of tears.

There is silence again. It is now quite dark apart from the light of the street-lamp in the centre. MICHAEL and MARTIN stand beneath it, heads bowed.)

MICHAEL Martin.

MARTIN What?

MICHAEL Do you reckon if we'd let Brian play with us he wouldn't have got run over and killed?

MARTIN I dunno ...

MICHAEL Jenny says them kids are all coming round tomorrow.

MARTIN I bet they want to go in our den to play that rudies again.

MICHAEL Yeah.

MICHAEL'S DAD *(Off-stage)* Michael! Martin! Get yourselves in now! It's dark and your mother wants you in!

MICHAEL *Coming*!

MICHAEL'S DAD Come on then, get a move on!

(Silence. They turn to go.)

MARTIN Shall we tell dad?

MICHAEL Don't know ... tell you what we can do tomorrow, though.

MARTIN What?

MICHAEL Take that den down!

MARTIN Yeah.

(MARTIN **and** MICHAEL **go off. The stage is empty. Lit only by the street-lamp. Silence. Suddenly, from the side we hear Brian's siren.** BRIAN **enters, riding his BMX, siren wailing. He stops in the centre, leaps off and faces upstage with feet apart and both hand thrust forward as if holding a gun.)**

BRIAN Alright! Come out with yer hands up! I've got you all surrounded!

(Silence. He turns rapidly to the right, then the left, then leaps round to point the 'gun' at the audience. Silence.)

BRIAN Orr, no I'll have to play with meself again now!!

(BRIAN kicks around a bit, then discovers the 'Beware of the Ferrit' sign lying on the ground.)

BRIAN Oh, great!

(Clutching the sign, BRIAN crosses to his bike and picks up an imaginary microphone from the handlebars.)

BRIAN Hallo! Tango Charlie Belta Zebra ... it's all clear! Yeah. I've got the evidence! I'm returning back to base now. Over and out!

(BRIAN hangs the sign round his neck. Leaps on his bike and rides off, siren wailing. Music comes on and the lights fade.)

The End

THE MAKING OF THE PLAY

Through teaching dramatic improvisation, I had often observed how fascinated pupils became in exploring their own childhood memories, and Hull Truck Youth Theatre provided the opportunity to try to form these ideas into a full-length play. In most cases, a novel, story or poem is written by an author working on his or her own, but theatre is a process involving many people working together. In the same way, producing a play script is often very different from other forms of writing – it certainly was with *Kidsplay*, where the young actors were involved from the beginning.

First of all, all of the cast were given responsibility for creating their own character, based on a young child they knew. These 'children' were then placed together in a wide variety of groupings and situations. The resulting improvisations flowed easily, just as children's games do. Relationships were made (and broken), pages of notes were taken and themes began to appear.

The most obvious of these was the clear class differences between different groups of children, obviously a result of their home backgrounds. This provided the possibility of conflict, which is vital to drama. The decision was then made to keep adults out of the story altogether, for this was to be a world they are no longer part of. They were represented through their children anyway, and would still remain the dramatic presence off-stage, always threatening to 'spoil the game'.

Some of these early scenes, such as the dolls' tea party in Act One, became part of the final script, but the work had to be given shape and structure if it was ever to become a real play. That is where the real writing process began. A great many settings had been used for all the background improvisations but deciding to fix the location in one place would not only avoid confusing scene changes but also help make the point that in the world of play a place can be anywhere a child wants it to be. It would also keep things clear for the audience since there would obviously be a great number of entrances and exits. The back-alley became the obvious setting – it was where kids play anyway; some could live directly off it and others could come from farther away. Family relationships were agreed to fit this pattern, starting with Michael and Martin as brothers in the centre house. Conflicting types were introduced by having Melanie next door throw a birthday party for her friends from dance class; and the final part of the story was provided by a common character that had emerged quite naturally – the kid *nobody* wants to play with, in this case, Brian Sullivan.

The acting workshops were then suspended for several weeks. This time was taken up with the difficult job of carefully planning the arrangement of all the entrances and exits necessary to provide organisation. This plan was used as the outline for more improvisation work on the separate scenes. Their order was experimented with again, a final form was chosen and important cue lines were fixed. So the spontaneous quality of the play was kept but everyone knew where they were going, when to enter and how and why to leave. Full rehearsals began, dialogue was eventually written out in full and an ending was inspired by the words of Edna St Vincent Millay: 'Childhood is the kingdom where nobody dies. Nobody that matters, that is.'

The final test, of course, was performance and, thankfully, audiences and critics seemed to find a sense of truth in what the play had to say. Whether reading or performing it, I hope you discover, or rediscover, some of the same reality of the lives of young children, or 'Kidsplay'.

John Lee

FOLLOW-UP ACTIVITIES

Casting the play

Kidsplay offers you different issues to consider when you are deciding who to cast for which part, because you are probably older than the characters of the play. Often, when older people play children, the performances tend to become caricatures; you can probably think of countless television shows, films and plays where this has happened. Sometimes it is intentional and meant to be comic. On other occasions, it gets in the way of what the production is trying to say. You will need to think hard about what style of presentation is suitable for this play. Having read the script carefully, you might like to make some notes to help your thinking:

- **Choose four or five characters and write detailed notes about them. John Lee, the playwright, has begun this for you with his short notes in the Cast List e.g.:**
  Michael (10) Likeable, cheeky, everybody's friend.
  What makes Michael likeable? Cheeky? Friendly? Look for the clues in the script. What sort of things might you look for in an actor to play this part (or the other parts that you have chosen)? Do you have someone in mind for the part? Why have you chosen him or her?
- **Choose a section of the play that you might ask someone to read in an audition. Write notes as to why you have chosen this piece and what you might be looking for in their reading that will help you to decide whether they are suitable for the part. Are there other things that you might ask your actor(s) to do? What performance skills might be needed?**

Writing and talking about the play: drama and childhood games

You may have played games as part of drama lessons. The links between childhood games, drama games and theatre are very obvious in this play and they are part of the pleasure of reading or watching the play. Were there games that you remembered as you went through the play for the first time? Did you find yourself thinking about other games you have played?

- **Think of a game that you often used to play. Write instructions for playing it and share this with a group to see if they can follow the rules. You may find that other people have played the game as well but have slightly different rules. As a way into working on the play practically you might like to run a couple of games sessions to explore old and new games. Can you incorporate some of them into this play? Do people who come from different places have different games?**
- **Sometimes, childhood games have chants that go with them. Skipping games often have a rhyme or an alphabet which decide all sorts of things about the people playing. How many can you remember? Write them down and see if anyone else remembers the same chants or if they have variations.**
- **Make up your own game and chant and try it out on a group of people. Does it work? Did you have to add rules to make it more difficult? Did you have to cut out rules to make it easier? It might be an idea to collect everybody's games together in a small booklet – there are often occasions such as drama lessons, holidays or just wet afternoons when it is fun to try new games.**
- **How many of the following games do you know or remember from your own past? Perhaps you could talk about them with a group? Are some of the people in the group you actually played the games with? Why were some games popular? (You may know some of these games under other names.)**
  Tig/Tag/Touch/He/Tugger, Chain He, Kingy, Poison, I Draw a Snake Upon Your Back, Chicken, Queenie, Mothers and Fathers, Playing School, Doctors and Nurses

Writing and talking about the play: memories

The playwright, John Lee, talks about the way the play was written as a group activity. Each actor contributed their own character and their own set of memories. There does seem to be something poignant or special about childhood memories. Elderly people often talk about the way in which they fail to recall things that they have done quite recently but can remember their childhood as if it were yesterday.

- **Think of things from your own childhood. Would they make good dramatic material? Try writing a short scene telling the story. If you are unsure about writing the episode as a dramatic scene, try writing it as a straight story first.**

- *Kidsplay* is set in Hull and many of the expressions and happenings described are very specific to the area. When we were publishing the play, we discussed the language of the play. Would people understand some of the terms if they were not familiar with Hull? Are there things that you don't understand? Find them and discuss them. Someone in your group might know what it means. What expressions do you remember that were specific to your childhood? Make a list and compare it with other people's. What words and sayings do you have in common? What differences are there? Ask your parents or older relatives about expressions, games and memories from their own childhood. Maybe they grew up somewhere very different from you.
- Nicknames are a strong tradition amongst children. Sometimes they are affectionate and friendly names. On other occasions they are very cruel and used to taunt, tease and bully. Sometimes they stick for a lifetime to the extent that real names get used rarely. Often the reason for the nickname itself gets forgotten. The children of *Kidsplay* talk of *Nitty Nora, the Bug Explorer*. She is one of the unseen, unheard adults of the play. How did she get this name? Why did she get called this name? Does she know about the name? Write an imaginative description of the woman and her life. How is she involved with the children of the play?

Improvisation and written drama work

- Think carefully about the characters of Michael and Martin, Shane and Charlotte or Melanie. Imagine clearly what their parents must be like. What clues are there in the script? Try casting the parts and acting out a scene in the house of one of the children when they go in at the end of the play.
- Either through improvisation or writing, create another scene for the play called *The Next Day*. You don't have to include all the characters in the play, but plan the timing of entrances carefully. Who appears first? Does Brian appear? When? How do the others react to him? Has anything changed? Compare your scenes with each other.

Producing the play

Most of the activities in this section have been about ideas and themes expressed in the play and not about creating a stage production. You might like to give this some thought. It may be that you are about to stage the play or scenes from the play. The structure of this play is a 'slice of life' – rather than a conventional storyline where something major happens that disrupts lives and needs to be resolved by the end of the play. This 'slice of life' feel to the play may make different demands of how you stage the play.

- **What stage set are you going to give to the piece? The action takes place in a *ten-foot* which is an alley behind a block of houses. Are you going to try and create a realistic set? What materials will you use to do this? Are you going to have a set at all. You could create the right feel for the play just using props such as boxes, bikes, bins and toys.**
- **Perhaps you just want to put on a scene from the play. Which one are you going to choose and why? Are you interested in a 'realistic' feel to the scene? Does the comedy of the piece appeal to you? How are you going to stage the scene? What sort of stage area are you going to use and how does this affect the relationship you want your actors to have with the audience? Do you want the audience to feel that they are almost looking at their own life being played out in front of them, or that they are looking in on other people's lives?**
- **Look carefully at the last scenes of the play from the point where Martin and Michael run on and Martin says:**
  Hey! Hey! There's been a road accident!
  Try out this section of the play (through to the end) with a group of actors paying very close attention to timing. Do pauses and a different pace of saying lines and acting things out change the feel of the scenes? What works best? How? Why? You might like to perform the options in front of a small audience and discuss with them what they feel about the scene. What do they like in the performance? What do they think could be improved?

Resource Reference: Iona and Peter Opie, *Children's Games in Street and Playground* (Oxford University Press, 1969).